Haffertee
Goes to School

Haffertee is a toy hamster. Ma
Diamond made him for her little girl,
Yolanda (usually known as Diamond
Yo), when her pet hamster died.

In this book – the fifth of the Haffertee
series – Haffertee decides to find out
what school is like. "It's a good place
for learning things," says Samson the
tortoise – and he's right. Haffertee
learns all sorts of things, and although
he's just a bit frightened at first he soon
makes friends and finds that school is
fun.

The charm of the stories lies in the
funny, lovable character of Haffertee
himself, and in the special place God
has in the affections of Diamond Yo
and her family.

The
Diamond
Family

Fran   Ma

Diamond Yo
with
Hafferree and
Howl Out

Pops

Mark

Chris.

Amy Lindon

Haffertee
Goes to School

Janet and John Perkins

A LION PAPERBACK
Oxford · Batavia · Sydney

Copyright © 1983 Janet and John Perkins
Illustrations copyright © 1983 Lion Publishing

Published by
Lion Publishing plc
Sandy Lane West, Littlemore, Oxford, England
ISBN 0 7459 1517 5
Lion Publishing Corporation
1705 Hubbard Avenue, Batavia, Illinois 60510, USA
ISBN 0 7459 1517 5
Albatross Books Pty Ltd
PO Box 320, Sutherland, NSW 2232, Australia
ISBN 0 7324 0025 2

First edition 1983
This edition 1989

Illustrations by Diane Matthes

Reproduced, printed and bound in Great Britain by
Hazell Watson & Viney Limited
Member of BPCC plc
Aylesbury, Bucks, England

Contents

It all began when Yo's pet hamster died. To cheer her up, Ma Diamond made a ginger-and-white toy hamster. The new Haffertee Hamster proved to be quite a character – inquisitive, funny and lovable. From his home in Yo's bedroom – shared with his friend Howl Owl and a strange collection of toys – he set out to explore Hillside House and meet the family: Ma and Pops Diamond and Yo's older brothers and sister, Chris, Fran and Mark. His adventures at home, at school and in the World Outside are told in six books of stories: *Haffertee Hamster, Haffertee's New House, Haffertee Goes Exploring, Haffertee's First Christmas, Haffertee Goes to School* and *Haffertee's First Easter.*

1

Samson the Tortoise has an Idea

Diamond Yo and Haffertee had spent nearly all the summer holidays exploring the World Outside.

They had been to the zoo and to the circus.

They had walked along the river bank and had a ride in a rowing-boat.

They had had two wonderful picnics down on the rocks under the cliff, and had spent a week in the sunshine in Cornwall.

It had been a fabulous holiday and they had loved it. Now it was all over. Today was the last day. Tomorrow it was back to school again for Diamond Yo.

Haffertee was beginning to feel rather funny inside. What could he do with himself while Yo was at school?

Howl Owl, his big barn-owl friend, who sat on the shelf above the door in Diamond Yo's room most of the time, was quite good at noughts and crosses.

Rabbearmonklio, the strange furry creature in the toy cupboard, could play dominoes very well.

Mr Jumpastring was very good at making up new songs. He was the little wooden man who hung about on a long piece of black elastic.

But all this seemed very dull compared with what Haffertee and Yo had been doing together during the holidays.

Tomorrow she was going to school without him. He began to feel just a little bit jealous as well as funny.

"What is so important about school?" he muttered to himself. "Why does Yo have to go?"

He didn't seem to be getting any answers, so he decided to go and see Samson the Tortoise.

Samson was very old and very clever. He lived in a bath tub in the garage during the winter and came out on to the grass in the front garden for the summer. He knew lots of answers.

Haffertee made his way out to the front garden to look for Samson. There was no sign of him at all.

Haffertee called his name: "SAMSON!"

There was no reply.

He began to look round – under the rose bushes and in among the flowers. Samson just wasn't there.

Haffertee was just going back into the house when he spotted a clump of long grass. He went over to it and looked in carefully. Samson was there, fast asleep.

Haffertee put his head right down close to the shell and shouted at the top of his voice: "SAMSON!!"

There was a slight movement and Samson poked out his head. His eyes were almost shut as he squinted in the bright sunlight.

"Oh!" he said, blinking hurriedly. "It's you, is it?" He didn't seem very pleased to have been awakened like that.

Haffertee waited as Samson pulled himself slowly out of the tall grass. He said he was sorry for shouting so, and then went on more softly.

"I would like to talk to you about school," he said.

"School!" said Samson. "Don't know much about school. Haven't been there for ages!"

"What's school like, then?" Haffertee asked. Surely Samson must be able to remember a little bit about it.

"Good place for learning things," said Samson, yawning sleepily. "Very good place for learning things."

Haffertee scratched his ear in a puzzled way. He didn't seem to be getting anywhere.

"But what do they *do* at school?" he went on.

"Ah!" said Samson, knowingly, and suddenly taking much more interest. "Now that's a different question altogether."

Haffertee closed his mouth tight shut. He *knew* that that was a different question altogether, but he did wish Samson would get on with it!

"They *do* all sorts of things," said Samson, reading Haffertee's thoughts. "They read books, they write stories, they do sums and they meet new friends. They draw things and make things and listen to things and dance round things and imagine things and sing things and play things and . . ."

"All right," said Haffertee, in a hurry. He felt almost out of breath listening to all that. It sounded very exciting indeed. "That's enough for now. Do you know any good hamster schools near here?"

Samson smiled. "No," he said, with a chuckle. "I'm afraid I don't."

"Oh," said Haffertee, very disappointed. "I was hoping I could go to one. I would love to do all those things."

Samson smiled again and began to chew his lip as he thought carefully about it all.

"Then why don't you ask Diamond Yo if

you can go to school with her tomorrow?" he said at last. "I'm sure she would be very pleased to take you."

Haffertee hadn't thought of that.

"What a good idea," he said. "What a *very* good idea. I'll go in and ask her straight away."

He turned, said Goodbye and Thank You to Samson and made his way back into the house.

Samson shuffled back down into the long grass again and went to sleep. One good idea a day was enough!

When Haffertee got back into the kitchen, he found Ma Diamond getting Yo's things ready for school.

Her uniform was neatly ironed and on a hanger.

Her special games clothes were in her bag and her running shoes were standing beside it.

Yo was trying on a big red apron with her name on it in white letters. She looked very smart.

Haffertee waited until the fussing and fitting was over. Then he said, "Er . . . Do you think I could go to school with you tomorrow?"

Yo looked at him in surprise.

"You really want to come to school with me tomorrow?"

Haffertee nodded. He was afraid she was going to say No.

"Why, yes," she said with a grin. "Certainly. That would be great!"

Ma Diamond smiled at them both.

"What a good idea," she said quickly. "I'll make a special pocket on the side of Yo's school bag and you can ride in that, Haffertee."

Haffertee was very excited. He could hardly wait. It would be just like the holiday all over again. Samson's idea was well worth having!

That night, at bedtime, when Yo said her prayers she added a special new one.

"Thank you, God, that Haffertee's starting school tomorrow. It will be fun having him with me."

She poggled Haffertee's ears, and he tingled with excitement as he snuggled down in the pillowcase by Yo's head.

2

The Apron and the Yammer Badge

Haffertee and Diamond Yo were a long time going to sleep. They were remembering all the fun they had had together during the summer holidays and thinking about all the things they were going to do at school. Yo knew just what to expect, but Haffertee wasn't quite so sure. Suddenly he began to feel just a little bit frightened.

There would be lots and lots of boys and girls, and he wouldn't know anyone.

There would be pushing and shoving and running and squashing in all that crowd.

He began to feel very small.

Samson knew all about school and Yo knew all about school. But Haffertee didn't know much about it at all. It was very confusing.

Yo seemed to have fallen asleep. Haffertee was all alone and wide awake. He began to feel worse and worse. There were so many strange new things about school that he didn't understand.

He decided to talk to Howl Owl.

He climbed slowly out of the pillowcase where he still slept at very exciting times and went over to Yo's desk.

"Howl," he called softly.

Howl heard, of course, because he was sitting up on the shelf above the door as usual. He fluttered down right next to his little friend.

"Why, Haffertee," he said in his very deep voice. "Whatever is the matter? You *do* look sad."

Haffertee struggled hard to keep back the tears, but he couldn't. He just had to stand there and let them come. They ran down his front fur in bobbles and plonked on to the desk.

"I'm frightened about going to school tomorrow," he sobbed. "It's all so strange and new and big and . . . not like home . . . and all day long . . . and . . . oh, Howl!"

Howl moved in close and put one wing gently round Haffertee's shoulders.

"It's an adventure," Howl said. "We all think you are very brave. But we stayed up late tonight just in case you felt a bit frightened. Being frightened on your own is not nice at all. Come on now, let's go into the toy cupboard."

He led Haffertee over to the cupboard and knocked on the door. It was opened slowly from the inside and it squeaked just as it always did.

The toy cupboard was full of Haffertee's friends.

Rabbearmonklio was hushing a little

baby doll to sleep.

Mr Jumpastring was singing and dancing and making everybody glad.

When Haffertee arrived, the hustle and bustle stopped.

Rabbearmonklio looked up from the cot. The baby doll was asleep.

"Haffertee!" he said with a great big smile. "Welcome to the toy cupboard again. We are all very glad to see you. We know that you are going to school tomorrow with Diamond Yo and we guessed you might be a bit scared. So we have something special to give you."

He moved away from the cot and came over to Haffertee. He was holding out a brightly-coloured parcel.

"This is for you, Haffertee," he said, holding out the parcel. "It's to remind you that you have lots of friends here. We'll all be thinking about you, especially tomorrow, and waiting to hear all about school when you get home."

Haffertee took the parcel and began to unwrap it. Inside was a red apron, just like Diamond Yo's, with his own name in big white letters on the front. All round the edges in spidery writing were the names of all his friends in the cupboard.

Haffertee put the apron on and then just stood there, not quite knowing what to say.

Diamond Yo suddenly poked her head round the door. She had missed him and come to see where he had gone.

"You do have a lot of friends," she said, merrily. "They all want to help you . . . and so do I. Look! Here is a Yammer Badge for you."

Haffertee looked. There was a square piece of stiff white cardboard in Yo's hand. On the front of it were some large red letters which said:

I YAMMER FRIEND OF
DIAMOND YO

Haffertee chuckled to himself as he struggled to pin the badge to his apron. He was feeling much better and all the tears had gone. He looked round at all his friends and gave each of them a big hug.

He said Goodbye and Thank You to them all. Then he went back into Diamond Yo's room.

It wasn't long before he was settled again in the pillowcase. Howl Owl sat quite still up on the shelf above the door, and Diamond Yo was snuggling back down into bed.

"We've both got aprons now," he said excitedly. "We certainly won't get lost, will we?"

Yo smiled into the darkness where she thought Haffertee would be.

"No," she said. "We certainly won't get lost!"

Haffertee wriggled a bit and then he said, "Have you got a Yammer Badge as well?"

Diamond Yo struggled with a yawn.

"Of course," she said sleepily. "Only mine says I YAMMER FRIEND OF HAFFERTEE. You are my friend and I am your friend. And Jesus is a friend of us both! So Good Night Haffertee. Sleep well! Tomorrow will be a super day."

And it was, of course.

3

The First Day

Even with Haffertee singing away merrily and Howl Owl hooting in her ear, Diamond Yo only just managed to wake up. It was so early!

The bed was warm and soft, and Diamond Yo was full of sleep. It was a long time before she could get her feet out on to the floor. She stretched and yawned and let out the sleep. Then she rubbed her eyes.

Haffertee was struggling into his apron, with the Yammer Badge still pinned on the front.

He managed to get the apron over his head and then straightened it. He looked splendid.

"I feel very safe," he said, "with my apron on like this. Everyone will know just who I am and who my friends are."

Diamond Yo tried to manage a smile and

began to move.

She went to the bathroom to wash. She cleaned her teeth carefully, and then started to get dressed. She looked very smart, too, in her uniform.

The two of them tumbled downstairs together for breakfast with the rest of the family. They were still scrunching and munching when Pops Diamond picked up a big fat book.

Haffertee knew what it was because Y had explained. It had B–I–B–L–E writte on the outside, and inside were stories abou God – the Great Maker and Jesus King.

Every morning Pops read a little bit of i out loud. Every day Yo and Haffertee were finding out more. They knew that God loved them and cared for them, just like Pops Diamond. And today they were glad when Pops said a special prayer, asking God to look after them on the First Day Back at School.

Family Hug Time came next and everyone gave each other a big hug. Then they set off for school.

Fran, Chris and Pops were going to the big school in the High Street.

Mark was going to the Junior School by Tower Farm.

And Ma Diamond was going up the hill to Hillcrest School with Yo and Haffertee.

Haffertee felt very important as he rode in the special pocket of Yo's school bag.

He watched carefully as more mothers

and children joined them, walking along the road.

He was just a little bit scared again when he saw the big crowd of children in the playground. One or two of them looked very sad as they waved Goodbye to their mothers.

Haffertee fingered his Yammer Badge and thought about all the names on his apron.

Ma Diamond patted him gently on the head and gave Yo a big kiss.

"'Bye," she said cheerfully. "See you this afternoon."

She walked off down the road and Haffertee and Yo went into the playground. They were together at school.

The school seemed to know they were coming. There was lovely bright green paint on the gate and on the fence. When they got inside they found that the classroom had been newly painted too. It was all fresh and bright.

Yo took Haffertee out of the pocket of the bag. Then she went into the classroom to find her special peg and to hang up her coat and the bag.

There was a big cardboard box in the

SPECIAL FRIENDS BOX

corner of the classroom. On one side of the box it said, in big stand-out letters, SPECIAL FRIENDS' BOX.

Yo put Haffertee in the box and then walked over to her table. Although there was a big door-hole in the box, Haffertee was beginning to feel lonely. But then he discovered there were several other Special Friends in the box already, and they made him feel better.

There was a well-worn teddy bear called Errington Wallbank. And there was a long green snuggly snake called Ann Gwiller. There was also a little fluffy monkey called Bong. He and Haffertee made friends straight away. They were about the same size and about the same colour – and they both looked very cheeky.

Yo had also found some of *her* friends. There was Mary Ellen who looked after Bong, and Tim Easton who always brought Errington Wallbank. They were busy talking together when a very cheerful looking lady came into the room.

It was Miss Bryland, the teacher.

All the talking and shuffling and sharing stopped.

"Good Morning, everyone," she said with a smile.

Haffertee found himself joining in the reply: "Good Morning, Miss Bryland."

"Welcome to you all," she said slowly. "And especially to those of you who are new to my class. Now will you please answer your names."

She began to read some names out of the register. Haffertee listened and tried hard to remember some of them. He was looking forward to meeting them during the day.

"Right," said Miss Bryland, when all the names had been called. "Let's go along to assembly."

Everyone set off down the long corridor

to the school hall.

There was some nice music coming from a brown box in the corner, and everyone seemed to be waiting for something – or rather some*one*.

It was Mrs Price, the Headmistress. Haffertee called her the Head Mischief for a long time that day until someone told him!

Mrs Price spoke for a little while and then one of the older boys read a story that Haffertee thought he had heard before. The singing that followed was bright and cheerful. Some of the children were playing flutes, blowing whistles, strumming guitars and banging drums.

Haffertee liked the sound very much. He decided that being at school was fun already!

The rest of the day was fun, too.

He played games with the class and listened to happy music.

He ran round the playground with Yo and talked to lots of new friends.

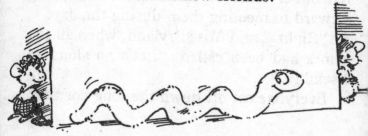

He had a great game of Hide-and-Seek with Bong and Errington Wallbank.

And he made all sorts of patterns with coloured beads and things.

His apron got covered in glue and paint, and he even rolled about on the floor like a seal.

It was all go-go-go and fun-fun-fun. It finished all too quickly. Ma Diamond met them at the gate and the three of them went home together.

What a day! What a lovely day! Haffertee was tired out. He only just managed his tea. Then he went upstairs to tell all his toy cupboard friends about the marvellous time he had had. Yo listened to all the excited chatter and added bits here and there. She was colouring a picture that Miss Bryland had given her.

At bedtime Yo had to speak quite firmly to Haffertee and Howl Owl. They took a long time to settle down.

Ma Diamond poked her head round the door.

"Jesus looked after you both very well, today, didn't he?" she said.

But there was no reply.

Everyone was asleep.

4

Not Quite So Good

Next day Miss Bryland was very pleased with the picture Yo had coloured. She put it on the display board straight away. It was a picture of a giraffe.

"Now then," she said, when the class was back from assembly, "I want you to copy this poem very carefully and learn it if you can."

She moved over to the blackboard and began to write on it with a little white stick. Haffertee watched in surprise as she did it. It was very clever to write like that!

"Off you go, then," said Miss Bryland when she had finished. "And try to copy it without any mistakes!"

Yo pulled a drawer from under her table and took out a book and a sharp pencil. She began to copy the poem from the board.

Haffertee climbed on to the table to

watch. She was doing very well. He couldn't see any mistakes at all.

"Can I try?" he asked at last, getting tired of sitting there and watching.

"Certainly," said Yo quickly, and she gave him a pencil and some paper and moved along the table to make room.

Haffertee picked up the pencil and started to write. He struggled to make the pencil go where he wanted it to go, but it wouldn't. It just wouldn't. It seemed to want to wander all over the paper and make wibbly wobbly lines.

Every now and then the sharp point stuck in the paper and turned Haffertee right round.

The writing wasn't writing at all. It was just a mess.

Haffertee grunted and puffed and struggled and strained. Then he threw down the pencil and stamped in disgust.

"Stupid pencil!" he muttered. "Stupid pencil!"

Miss Bryland came over to the table to see what was the matter.

"Well now, Haffertee," she said. "What seems to be the trouble?"

Haffertee frowned.

"The pencil is stupid," he shouted. "It won't do what I want it to do. It gets in between my legs and trips me up," he said angrily. "Sometimes it gets behind my head and knocks me over. It even gets under my arms and tickles me and makes me laugh. That's why my writing is all Higgledee-Piggledee-OOOOps. This pencil is useless. I'm not going to do any more silly writing!"

Miss Bryland waited till he had finished. Then she said quite firmly. "You must finish your work before you go out to play."

Haffertee could feel himself getting all cross and worked up inside.

"Stay in here while Yo and my friends play outside?" he thought. The idea was terrible. "I won't do it!" he said fiercely. "I *won't* do it!"

Miss Bryland picked up the pencil. She turned it over and over in her hand.

"I think this pencil is too long for you, Haffertee," she said, at last. "Try this one. It's shorter."

Haffertee hesitated for a moment. Then he reached out and took the shorter pencil.

"Now then," said Miss Bryland quite sternly. "Try again!"

Haffertee was feeling terrible inside, but he held on to his temper and began to write.

His writing was still untidy at first but then very slowly it got better and better, and he was soon writing smoothly. It was very much easier with the shorter pencil.

"That's good," said Miss Bryland, when he had finished the first line. "Very good. Now finish the verse and then you can go out to play."

Haffertee wasn't very pleased about that but he went on copying carefully until the verse was done. Miss Bryland stayed with him all the time and encouraged him as he went along.

"There now," she said, when he had finished, "that's much better. There are ten minutes of playtime left. Off you go!"

Haffertee didn't need to be told twice. He shot out of the room and into the playground.

Diamond Yo was waiting for him.

"Did you do it?" she called as he ran past. "Did you do it?"

Haffertee skidded to a stop, turned and nodded.

"Yes," he said with a flicker of a smile. "Just about."

"Good for you," said Diamond Yo. "Good for you. Miss Bryland is very strict but she is also very fair. She expects us to do our best and she doesn't like it if we don't try hard. But if you really get stuck she always listens and tries to help. She is a very nice teacher."

Haffertee wasn't quite so sure. He had only a few minutes left to play.

When he got back to the classroom his writing was gone. He couldn't see it anywhere. He began to be worried.

"It's all right, Haffertee," said Miss Bryland as she came in and saw him searching around. "It's up there!"

She nodded towards the display boards on the wall.

"There. Next to Yo's picture of the giraffe."

Haffertee looked. It was there, sure enough. The first verse of the poem.

What a neck, so long, so bendy and strong.
Reaching right up to the sky.
Touching the clouds and brushing the wind.
Towering giraffe going by.

Haffertee *was* pleased.

He was bursting to tell his friends what had happened when he got home, and when Pops heard about it he was delighted. He went up to Yo's room at bedtime and gave

Yo a big hug and a kiss. He picked Haffertee up carefully and stroked his front fur.

"Well done, Haffertee," he said with a smile. "Well done. School can be quite hard sometimes but if you stick at your work and keep trying you will be all right."

He tucked Haffertee gently into the pillowcase and turned to go out.

"God bless you both," he said, as he switched off the light. "Good Night and God bless!"

5

Don't Forget the Doodoos

Getting up and going off to school was a bit of a rush. On the first Wednesday morning of the term it was a terrible scramble.

Everything went wrong.

The alarm clock didn't alarm and so Pops Diamond was very late getting up.

That meant that everybody else was very late getting up. Someone left the soap in the water and it was all soggy. Yo trod on the toothpaste tube and it squirted all over the floor.

She couldn't find one of her socks because Smudge Purrswell had shuffled off with it.

Haffertee's apron had fallen down between the bed and the wall and he had a terrible job getting it out.

Ma Diamond burned the toast twice and Fran banged her toe against the chair.

It was one of those dreadful mornings!

Yo was still crunching toast as she set off for school with Haffertee and Ma Diamond.

Haffertee was puffing a lot as he settled into the special pocket of Yo's bag.

Just as they arrived at the school gates he remembered something, and got all in a panic.

"Oh!" he shouted. "We've forgotten Gary Lee's clothes!"

Yo laughed and spluttered.

"Not Gary Lee's clothes, Haffertee," she said. "Galilee clothes! Galilee clothes!"

She turned quickly to Ma and began to explain.

"Miss Bryland wants us to look like people in Galilee this morning. We are going to do a play in assembly about a great crowd of people being given a picnic by Jesus, and she has asked us to bring some clothes to dress up with."

Ma Diamond frowned. There was no time now to go home and sort clothes like that. What *could* they do? She stood there quite still for a moment, thinking. Perhaps Mrs Thompson, who lived across the road from the school, would help.

"Wait here a minute," she said quickly. "I'll go and see what I can do."

She walked carefully across the road to Mrs Thompson's house and went in. When she came back she had a plastic bag full of materials. Mrs Thompson had been very kind and was pleased to help.

Ma Diamond went on into school with Haffertee and Yo to tell Miss Bryland why they were so late.

Miss Bryland wasn't cross at all. She asked Ma if she would like to stay to see the play in assembly. It was great fun. And

Haffertee and Yo looked splendid in their coloured Galilee coats.

Then everyone settled down to a full day of things to do . . . stories to write, poems to learn, books to read, sums to work out, music to hear and games to play. Haffertee and Yo soon forgot all about the rush and scramble of the early morning.

Ma Diamond met them as usual at the school gate. She had been to the paper shop to buy a sheet of thick white plastic and two felt pens.

As they walked home she told them what she was going to do.

43

"I'll ask Pops to fix this plastic sheet somewhere on the wall of the kitchen where we can all reach it," she said. "Then, when we come home in the evening we can write down all the things that we have to remember for the next day and get them ready before bedtime. Things like dinner money and special clothes and pencils and gym shoes. We don't want to have to scramble about in the morning like that again."

Haffertee and Yo nodded. They liked the idea and said so.

When Pops arrived later, Ma asked him to fix the plastic board in place and he set to work with his drill and screwdriver.

When it was all done, Haffertee began to write some great big letters on the board:

D O O D O O s

"Doodoos," said Pops in surprise. "What on earth are doodoos?"

Yo chuckled.

"The cardboard tube in the middle of a toilet roll is a doodoo," she said firmly. "They make super trumpets! Miss Bryland says that we shall need some trumpets when we do a play about Joshua in assembly next week. She told us that God helped the people to blow hard and to shout loud so that the walls of Jericho fell down!"

Pops smiled, imagining the whole class stomping round blowing doodoos.

"The Bible really seems to come alive in your school," he said merrily.

Yo smiled back.

"Yes," she said. "It's full of good stories."

She turned to look for Haffertee. He was going through the door on his way upstairs.

"I'm going to make sure that everything is ready for tomorrow. I don't want to have to chase around in the morning again."

"And I'll make sure the toothpaste stays in the tube tomorrow," said Yo, as she followed him up to her room.

6

Haffertee Kicks the Castle

Haffertee and Bong the monkey had been friends from the very first day at school. They got on very well together. They were about the same size. And they both loved lively music. At movement and dance they were the best in the class. They could make themselves into tall trees waving their arms in the air or into small field mice curled up in a hole.

But when it came to making things it was difficult.

Bong could make anything.

Haffertee was all thumbs.

Nothing he made stayed together for long. It always fell apart. That's what happened on Thursday.

Thursday afternoon is Craft afternoon.

It's the afternoon for sticking things together and sewing things up and bending wires and building houses. The things the class had to make today were castles, crowns and royal robes.

Miss Bryland had been reading to them about kings and queens. So this afternoon everyone had to make something "royal".

Bong and Haffertee were building castles with coloured bricks.

Bong's castle was just right. The walls were thick and firm. The tower was straight and tall. The drawbridge looked just like a real one and the gate fitted perfectly.

Haffertee's castle was . . . oh dear! The walls were thin and shaky. The tower was crooked and dumpy. The drawbridge had fallen into the moat and the gate was far too big to fit.

Bong's castle looked good.

Haffertee's castle looked dreadful.

Haffertee was very upset. All of a sudden he threw his bricks into the air and stamped his feet on the floor.

"It's not fair," he shouted. "It's just not fair!"

Bong looked up. He was just putting the finishing touches to Castle Bong.

Haffertee stood there for just a moment

longer. Then he walked over to Castle Bong and kicked it!

The coloured bricks shot up in the air and all over the room.

Haffertee was very angry.

Bong stood up slowly, looked fiercely at Haffertee, and then, with a terrible yell, jumped on him!

There was a mixed-up, turning, twisting bundle of fur rolling about on the floor. It was screeching and grunting and puffing and groaning. It banged against the legs of tables and chairs and it rolled into corners. It was a terrible fight.

Miss Bryland came running over and pulled the two of them apart. It was over as quickly as it had begun.

They both looked like very sorry little creatures.

Their fur was all over the place and they were out of breath. Haffertee's ear was torn and Bong's tail had come off. It was on the floor near the door.

They were both very near to tears.

Miss Bryland carried them up to her table while the rest of the class watched in silence.

"All right now," she said to them all. "This has been a nasty fight. Let's see if we can sort it out together."

The class sat quiet and still, waiting.

"You two are usually the best of friends," she said slowly. "Please tell me what happened."

Haffertee looked at Bong and Bong looked at Haffertee. They both began to talk at once.

"One at a time, please!" said Miss Bryland.

Haffertee looked at Bong again and he nodded for him to go on.

"Well," said Haffertee, shuddering suddenly. "You told us to make a castle and I tried very hard. But it just wouldn't work. When I saw Bong's lovely castle I didn't feel good at all."

Haffertee hung his head.

"So . . .," said Miss Bryland firmly, "what did you do?"

"I-threw-down-my-bricks-and-I-kicked-his-castle," said Haffertee, all in one breath.

"Is that all?" said Miss Bryland. She looked now as though she was almost smiling.

"No," said Haffertee, gathering speed for the second time. "I kicked it again and threw the bricks up in the air. I was so angry that I kicked Bong as well!"

Bong waved his hands. "Then I got angry, too," he said, "and we started to fight."

"Yes," said Miss Bryland firmly. "I know that. And now look at you."

Haffertee and Bong hung their heads.

"Well," said Miss Bryland at last, after taking some deep breaths. "None of us can be good at everything, Haffertee. But we should be pleased when other people do things well. You were wrong to spoil Bong's castle and you must say sorry."

Haffertee gulped.

"Sorry," he muttered, looking at the floor.

"Not like that, Haffertee," said Miss Bryland. "Say it properly and mean it."

Haffertee swallowed hard. Saying sorry was bad enough. Saying it and meaning it was even worse. He lifted his head with a great effort and looked straight into Bong's eyes.

Bong was his friend. And he'd kicked down his castle and torn off Bong's tail! Suddenly Haffertee felt ashamed of himself. He was really truly sorry. He wanted so much to be friends again.

"I'm sorry, Bong," he said. "I lost my temper. I'm sorry I kicked your castle. And I'm sorry I hurt you. Please forgive me."

Bong smiled.

"That's all right," he said. "I'm sorry I jumped on you."

They stood there facing each other for a moment or so and then Miss Bryland spoke again.

"Friends?" she asked.

"Yes," said Haffertee. "Friends again." And he walked over to Bong and gave him a hug.

Diamond Yo smiled.

Miss Bryland sighed.

The rest of the class went back to Craft.

7

Heads, Hands and Feet

Haffertee's ear and Bong's tail were mended when they met again on Friday morning. They both felt much better for a good night's sleep.

Miss Bryland came into the room with a big roll of black paper under her arm. Everyone wondered what it was.

As soon as assembly was over, Miss Bryland sat down and smoothed out the roll of paper across her table. She took a pair of scissors from her drawer and began to cut the black paper into pieces. The whole class watched in surprise.

"It's heads, hands and feet this morning," she said with a smile.

"Heads, hands and feet," whispered Haffertee to Bong. "Whatever does she mean?"

Bong put his hands in the air, palms up,

and shrugged his shoulders. He didn't understand it at all.

"I want you to write your names on these, please," said Miss Bryland, and she pulled a pile of small white cards from her drawer and put them on the table. "Then, when I call your name, I would like you to come out here to me and I will draw the outline of your head on a piece of black paper."

Haffertee chuckled and felt the fur on the top of his head. It will be quite hard to draw an outline of that, he thought. Then he looked at Ann Gwiller, the long green snake. She had a very funny-shaped head and Haffertee was sure Miss Bryland couldn't draw that.

While he was doing all this thinking, Miss Bryland had taken out the register and was finding the right page.

"While I am drawing the outlines up here," she said, "I would like you to put one hand flat on to a piece of paper and ask the boy or girl next to you to draw round the outside. Do it carefully, finger by finger. Then come and show me when you have finished. After that I want you to do the

same with your foot as well. Of course you
will have to take off your shoe and sock!"
There were smiles all round the room. This
sounded like great fun.

"When we've done all that," said Miss
Bryland, "we can put all the heads and

hands and feet on the walls round the room. Then we shall see how very different we all are."

Haffertee started straight away, writing his name very carefully on the piece of white card that Yo gave him. She drew round his hand and then round his foot.

Miss Bryland went on calling out names and drawing head outlines as fast as she could. She was working very hard.

"Haffertee," she called. "It's your turn now."

Haffertee went up to the front and sat down on the table. Miss Bryland began to draw his head.

She was very clever and soon had a good picture of Haffertee from the side. He showed her the outline of his hand and foot and she ticked them for him. He went back to his place.

"Now then," said Miss Bryland at last. "You can all go out to play."

Diamond Yo and four or five other boys and girls stayed behind to help with the cutting and some very fast pasting. They managed to get all the outlines up on the wall before it was time for the others to come back.

Miss Bryland put up all the name cards with the letters facing the wall so that no one could read them.

Playtime for the rest of the class seemed longer than usual. Everyone wanted to get back into the classroom to see all the heads and hands and feet. It was quite a sight.

There were heads with long hair and heads with short hair.

There were long noses and short noses and snub noses and one broken nose.

There were foreheads that sloped back and foreheads that sloped forward.

Thick heads, thin heads, long heads and fat heads. All shapes and sizes. It was marvellous.

Haffertee couldn't believe his eyes. Every head was different.

The hands and feet were all a bit different, too, and there were no names to help.

"We'll have a competition now," said Miss Bryland, "and see who can recognize the biggest number of other boys and girls just from those outlines."

It was great fun.

Haffertee didn't do very well at all, although everybody was able to recognize *his* hand and foot. He was very surprised at all the differences.

He couldn't stop talking about them when he got home.

"Are we really so different?" he asked, when he and Yo were getting ready for bed. "Really so very different?"

"We certainly are," said Yo, as she climbed in. "When God made people, he made everyone different and special. He knows everything about us too."

Haffertee thought about that quietly for a moment or so as he snuggled down into the pillowcase.

"Can he recognize me from the outline of my head?" he asked.

"Yes," said Yo. "I'm sure he can. Anybody could recognize *your* head. He certainly knows your name."

"My word!" said Haffertee. "He must have a good register!"

Yo chuckled.

"Go to sleep," she said. "Go to sleep!"

8

Haffertee Gets in a Mess

Haffertee's head became famous all round the school. Children came into Miss Bryland's classroom just to see how well she had drawn him.

Haffertee had settled in and was enjoying everything about school. When Saturday came he was very disappointed that there was no school!

As the weeks went by, he watched Yo learn to swim in the Backwelton Indoor Pool.

He cheered her on when she played hopscotch.

He learned to play the tin whistle all by himself, and he stayed behind on Mondays for Band Practice when Yo was with the choir.

His counting was getting better and his writing was getting neater.

He could read quite well and he was beginning to learn how to make things that didn't fall apart.

He had lots of friends and he loved being at school.

The time was going very fast.

Then, on the day before the Harvest Festival, he disappeared.

At morning assembly that day, Mrs Price talked about harvest. "God made the wonderful world we live in," she said, "and tomorrow, in the Harvest Festival, we shall thank him together."

What she said next made them all think hard.

"And we will ask him to help us share what we have. There are so many hungry people in the world today!"

Haffertee was talking about what Mrs Price had said right up to dinner time.

After dinner there was no sign of him.

He had just disappeared.

Miss Bryland looked for him everywhere.

Mrs Price asked four of the older boys to look very carefully all round the school.

Nobody could find Haffertee.

Yo couldn't understand it. He was so happy at school that she was quite sure he hadn't run away.

Ma Diamond couldn't understand it when she arrived to take them home. She looked round the school herself but she didn't find Haffertee either.

He was gone!

Yo was very sad to have to go home without her little soft-toy friend and when she got to her room she asked God to take care of Haffertee, wherever he was.

Howl Owl and the friends in the toy

cupboard were all very upset. So was the whole Diamond family.

Pops Diamond decided to go up to the school with Chris and Mark to have one last look round before it got too dark. As they turned into the school playground, there was the pig-food truck. A farmer who lived close to the school came every evening to collect all the food that was left over from the dinners. He gave it to his pigs. There was a metal bin outside the door of the kitchens and the school cook put all the scraps in there.

Pops and Chris and Mark sat in the car, wondering where to start their search.

Mr Briggs, the farmer, took the lid off the bin and then stood quite still looking down into it. He had seen something very strange.

Pops jumped out of the car and ran over to see what it was. Chris raced to the bin and just managed to beat Mark.

Mr Briggs was pulling Haffertee out.

He was in a terrible mess. He was covered in mashed potatoes and gravy and custard, and he smelled funny.

Pops took the bedraggled little figure gently from the farmer and went inside the school. Mrs Posset the caretaker was still there and she unlocked the Staff Room. Very gently Pops washed Haffertee in warm water and then dried him with paper towels.

Haffertee was beginning to look more like Haffertee! But he didn't speak at all and he seemed very sorry for himself.

"We'll take him home now," said Pops. "He's had a nasty time. But perhaps when he sees Yo and his other friends from the toy cupboard he will begin to feel better."

When Haffertee arrived back in Diamond Yo's room everyone was delighted to see him and to have him home again.

They all waited patiently until Haffertee felt like talking. Then they listened very carefully to what he had to say. He began very slowly . . . it was a long story.

"I listened to what Mrs Price said about food for hungry people and about the Harvest Festival," he said. "And I thought of all those hungry children in other countries.

Then at dinner time I heard the boys and girls complaining about school dinners. One didn't want any meat. Another said the gravy was too thick. One boy grumbled about the skin on his custard. And his friend complained because he hadn't any. 'This apple pie doesn't look anything like my Mum's apple pie,' one little girl said. 'I don't like it.'

"It made me sad. After dinner I went to the back of the kitchen to see what happened to all the food that was left on the plates. They tipped it into the bin. I went a bit closer and climbed up on the edge to see how much there was. Then when I was standing on the edge I slipped and fell, and the lid came down over me. I shouted at the top of my voice but no one heard. I shouted the names of all my friends on the apron. But no one came and I didn't know what to do next. Then I remembered that God knew where I was and I stopped being frightened. I knew he would send someone to help. And I was *so* pleased when he told Mr Briggs, and Pops and Chris and Mark."

It was a very long story and Haffertee told it with a good many gulps and sniffs.

When it was all over he was very tired.

Ma Diamond brought him some of his favourite banana sandwiches and a glass of milk. When he had finished, Yo tucked him away in the pillowcase and settled down beside him in her bed.

Howl Owl went to his shelf and all the others returned to the toy cupboard.

"Oh, Haffertee," said Yo, fluffing his fur gently. "I am so glad you're back."

"So am I," said Haffertee weakly. "So am I."

9

The Band Practice

The last week of the Christmas term is always exciting. There are so many things to do.

At Hillcrest School there were decorations to make for the hall and classrooms, stars for every window and golden bells for every ceiling. A great Christmas tree

appeared in the hall with pretty coloured lights blinking on and off, and a growing pile of parcels underneath.

There was a final collection of milk-bottle tops. (The school was helping to pay for a guide dog for a blind man who lived near by.)

Haffertee was allowed to take two of his friends with him on special invitation for the last week. Howl Owl and Mr Jumpastring were really delighted to join in all that was going on.

Wednesday came – the day of the concert. Lots of grown-ups were invited to school in the afternoon for a cup of tea and some cakes.

Ma Diamond was coming in to help with the teas and Pops was coming later, just to be there for the concert. Haffertee was going to play his tin whistle and the school band was going to play Christmas music. They had all been practising their songs and poems for weeks.

It was at the final practice that the fun began!

It took place in the hall immediately after dinner. The members of the band were waiting outside, ready to come in when they were called.

Mr Roberts, the conductor, went to the door and blew a very funny motor hooter. It was a strange sound, but those in the band knew just what it meant. They came running in and took their places in the hall. Then they began to play their instruments.

What happened next is hard to explain.

The boy who was playing the trumpet just could not get a sound out of it. He blew and blew and blew and went redder and redder and redder, until he just had to stop. Then he found that *someone* had blocked up his trumpet with wet newspaper!

The children playing the triangle didn't get a ringing note at all. Just a solid plop. *Someone* had put sticky plaster on the strikers and on the triangles.

The guitars sounded very dull. There were tissues in the sound boxes!

When the violins started, they rattled. They were full of peanuts!

Poor Mr Roberts didn't know whether to laugh, or to shout, or to walk out. Instead he picked up his baton and tapped it against the table.

It fell to pieces in his hand and dropped to the floor in front of him.

It was all a trick!

Slowly at first, and then growing like a great wave, the smiles turned to chuckles and the chuckles turned to laughter. Getting louder and louder, surging through the hall like some great music. Everyone was laughing and falling about. The whole hall was shaking with laughter.

Haffertee had a good laugh himself. But he was rather anxious to get on with the practice and to try his tin whistle solo.

At last all the instruments were back to normal and they played through one or two pieces until they came to the place for Haffertee and his whistle.

He took a deep breath ready to begin, blew his whistle gently to make the notes, and . . . bubbles . . . bubbles . . . bubbles.

They came slipping and sliding out of the end. Someone had filled his whistle with bubble mixture! The bubbles floated about all over the place.

Haffertee didn't quite know what to do.

Howl Owl and Mr Jumpastring were holding their sides with laughter. It really hurt! There was no doubt now who was responsible for all the tricks!

The band practice eventually got going properly and after all that muddle everything was fine. When the grown-ups came to school they were given a magnificent tea and they listened to the band and to the solos and the poems. They *did* enjoy them. When it was all over they clapped and clapped and clapped. The concert was a great success. Everyone was ready to burst with happiness.

When Haffertee got home that night he decided to have a few words with Howl Owl and Mr Jumpastring. He wasn't really cross about their jokes because everything had gone so well – so the words didn't last very long.

"Don't worry, Haffertee," said Mr Jumpastring. "No one was hurt. It was just a good Christmas joke. Christmas is a time for fun and happiness, you know."

Haffertee did know. He had done a lot of detective work for his first Christmas – and he knew just who it was who made it such a happy time!

It was Jesus, the baby whose birthday we enjoy each Christmas time.

10
A Bag Full of Buttons

Haffertee was busy, carefully brushing his fur.

Today was a very special day.

It was the last day of term.

The classrooms were going to be open for the Mums and Dads to see all the work that had been done:

– the poems and stories they had written;

– the pictures they had drawn and coloured;

– the models and shapes they had made, and the books the children had been reading.

Haffertee really wanted to take Samson to school to show him everything and to let him meet his new friends.

But Samson had got very, very sleepy a week or two after Haffertee had started school. So Pops Diamond had tucked him away snugly among the folds of an old coat in an old-fashioned bath tub at the back of the garage. He couldn't be disturbed till winter was over.

"Come on, Haffertee!" shouted Diamond Yo as she rushed down the stairs. "We shall be late for breakfast."

Haffertee wondered just how many times he had heard that!

He finished brushing and started downstairs after Yo. The family had breakfast together and then listened as Pops read a story from the Bible. Today it was about ten people who were healed by Jesus. But only one of them went back to say Thank You.

Pops closed the Bible and then pulled out two small bags from under the table. One was red and one was green. He had been hiding them on his lap.

"Haffertee and Yo," he said slowly, "I want you to take these two bags to school with you today. The red one is full of buttons and the green one is empty. Every time you find something to say Thank You for, I want you to take a button out of the red bag and put it into the green bag."

Haffertee thought that was a very good

idea, and he said so.

"We're coming to school this afternoon," said Pops. "Then you can tell me how you've got on."

Family Hug Time came and went and Haffertee settled down into the pocket in Yo's school bag.

"That's the first button," he said, merrily. "We must put one in the green bag for this very nice seat for me to ride in!"

Ma Diamond smiled. She walked up the road with them and left them at the gate. The two of them went into school together.

"Look!" said Haffertee, happily. "That little girl cried when she first came to school. She is quite happy now. That's another button."

They went inside together, thinking about Thank You buttons. Yo put her coat and bag on her peg while Haffertee went to the Special Friends' Box.

"It's lovely and warm in here," said Yo, "so there's another button. That's three already!"

She put the two coloured bags down on her table and took three buttons out of the red one and rattled them into the green one. It was great fun!

And so it went on right through the day. They put buttons into the green bag every time they saw something (or someone) and wanted to say Thank You.

There was a button for Miss Bryland because she was strict and kind.

There was one for Haffertee's writing and one for Diamond Yo's picture.

There was one for playtime and one for the school cook.

There was one for bricks for building castles and one for elastic bands and nails for making shapes.

There was one for Bong and one for Ann Gwiller.

There was one for the school band.

Another and another and another.

The two of them spent the whole day saying Thank You for something or Thank You to someone.

Miss Bryland thought it was such a good idea that she cut out some buttons from coloured card and sent an older boy to the sweet shop down the road to buy some bags.

The whole class was full of Thank You buttons.

Pops Diamond really had started something.

It was a wonderful last day of term. At the end of the afternoon there was some lovely Christmas music and singing. And they had stories and poems about the baby Jesus in Bethlehem.

Everyone was happy and sad at the same time.

Happy because the holidays were coming and sad because school was over and they had to leave so many good friends.

"Now," said Mrs Price at last, "before you go home, one special Thank You to Jesus for making all this possible. Without him there would be no Christmas at all."

Haffertee smiled. He knew she was

right. He had looked at Christmas very carefully last year when he had first bumped into it. (You can read what happened in *Haffertee's First Christmas*.)

Then it was home time, and the whole Diamond family thanked God together for a very happy term.

Haffertee spent most of the evening talking excitedly to his friends.

Just as he was getting ready for bed, he turned to Diamond Yo.

"Look," he said, "I've still got three buttons left. There's one for Samson and his good idea. Without that I would never have gone to school. There's one for you for being my very best friend. And there's a Thank You to God for making school such fun."

Yo smiled and sighed.

"Haffertee," she said. "You are a smasher!"

Haffertee chuckled as he dropped the last three buttons into the green bag.

He snuggled down into the pillowcase.

His first term at school was over.

The green bag was full.

More stories from LION PUBLISHING for you to enjoy:

YOUNG LION STORY BOOKS

THE DAY THE FAIR CAME - AND OTHER STORIES		£1.50 ☐
UNDER THE GOLDEN THRONE	Ralph Batten	£1.25 ☐
HAFFERTEE HAMSTER	Janet and John Perkins	£1.25 ☐
HAFFERTEE'S NEW HOUSE	Janet and John Perkins	£1.25 ☐
HAFFERTEE GOES EXPLORING	Janet and John Perkins	£1.25 ☐
HAFFERTEE'S FIRST CHRISTMAS	Janet and John Perkins	£1.25 ☐
HAFFERTEE GOES TO SCHOOL	Janet and John Perkins	£1.25 ☐
HAFFERTEE'S FIRST EASTER	Janet and John Perkins	£1.25 ☐

All Lion paperbacks are available from your local bookshop or newsagent, or can be ordered direct from the address below. Just tick the titles you want and fill in the form.

Name (Block Letters)

Address

. . . .

Write to Lion Publishing, Cash Sales Department, PO Box 11, Falmouth, Cornwall TR10 9EN, England.

Please enclose a cheque or postal order to the value of the cover price plus:

UK: 60p for the first book, 25p for the second book and 15p for each additional book ordered to a maximum charge of £1.90.

OVERSEAS: £1.25 for the first book, 75p for the second book plus 28p per copy for each additional book.

BFPO: 60p for the first book, 25p for the second book plus 15p per copy for the next seven books, thereafter 9p per book.

Lion Publishing reserves the right to show on covers and charge new retail prices which may differ from those previously advertised in the text or elsewhere, and to increase postal rates in accordance with the Post Office.